Too Cute!
Baby Bears

by Christina Leaf

BELLWETHER MEDIA
MINNEAPOLIS, MN

Blastoff! Beginners are developed by literacy experts and educators to meet the needs of early readers. These engaging informational texts support young children as they begin reading about their world. Through simple language and high frequency words paired with crisp, colorful photos, Blastoff! Beginners launch young readers into the universe of independent reading.

Sight Words in This Book

a	from	like	so	up
are	have	look	the	
at	he	one	there	
big	help	out	they	
come	in	play	this	
find	is	she	to	

This edition first published in 2022 by Bellwether Media, Inc.

No part of this publication may be reproduced in whole or in part without written permission of the publisher. For information regarding permission, write to Bellwether Media, Inc., Attention: Permissions Department, 6012 Blue Circle Drive, Minnetonka, MN 55343.

Library of Congress Cataloging-in-Publication Data

Names: Leaf, Christina, author.
Title: Baby bears / by Christina Leaf.
Description: Minneapolis, MN : Bellwether Media, 2022. | Series: Blastoff! beginners: Too cute! | Includes bibliographical references and index. | Audience: Ages 4-7 | Audience: Grades K-1
Identifiers: LCCN 2021001445 (print) | LCCN 2021001446 (ebook) | ISBN 9781644874844 (library binding) | ISBN 9781648344664 (paperback) | ISBN 9781648343926 (ebook)
Subjects: LCSH: Bears--Infancy--Juvenile literature.
Classification: LCC QL737.C27 L3975 2022 (print) | LCC QL737.C27 (ebook) | DDC 599.7813/92--dc23
LC record available at https://lccn.loc.gov/2021001445
LC ebook record available at https://lccn.loc.gov/2021001446

Text copyright © 2022 by Bellwether Media, Inc. BLASTOFF! BEGINNERS and associated logos are trademarks and/or registered trademarks of Bellwether Media, Inc.

Editor: Amy McDonald   Designer: Jeffrey Kollock

Printed in the United States of America, North Mankato, MN.

Table of Contents

A Baby Bear!	4
Out of the Den	12
All Grown Up!	20
Baby Bear Facts	22
Glossary	23
To Learn More	24
Index	24

A Baby Bear!

Look at the baby bear!
Hello, cub!

Cubs are born in **dens**. They come out in spring.

den

Cubs **nurse**.
They drink milk
from mom.

Most cubs
have one
brother or sister.

Out of the Den

Cubs play together! They like to **wrestle**.

wrestling

Cubs like
to climb.
Hello up there!

Mom helps cubs find food.
They find berries.

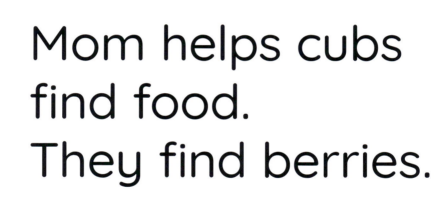

berries

This cub hunts.
She got a fish!

All Grown Up!

This cub is one.
He is a **yearling**.
He is so big!

Baby Bear Facts

Bear Life Stages

cub yearling adult

A Day in the Life

climb find food wrestle

Glossary

dens

homes for some animals

nurse

to drink mom's milk

wrestle

to fight by holding and pushing

yearling

a bear older than one year but not fully grown

To Learn More

ON THE WEB

FACTSURFER

Factsurfer.com gives you a safe, fun way to find more information.

1. Go to www.factsurfer.com.

2. Enter "baby bears" into the search box and click 🔍.

3. Select your book cover to see a list of related content.

Index

bear, 4	hunts, 18
berries, 16	milk, 8
born, 6	mom, 8, 16
brother, 10	nurse, 8, 9
climb, 14	play, 12
dens, 6	sister, 10
drink, 8	spring, 6
fish, 18	wrestle, 12, 13
food, 16	yearling, 20, 21

The images in this book are reproduced through the courtesy of: Eric Isselee, front cover, pp. 3, 4, 12 (left, right); Rosa Jay, p. 5, 22 (cub); Lars Ove Jonsson, p. 6; blickwinkel/ Alamy, pp. 6-7; Sergey Uryadnikov, pp. 8-9, 12-13, 23 (yearling); Volodymyr Burdiak, pp. 10-11; Agnieszka Bacal, pp. 14-15; Scisetti Alfio, p. 16; Jim Cumming, pp. 16-17; Egor Clasov, pp. 18-19; robertharding/ Alamy, pp. 20-21; DPS, p. 22 (yearling); Sashluk, p. 22 (adult); jo Crebbin, p. 22 (climb); Giedriius, p. 22 (food); Kireeva Veronika, p. 22 (wrestle); Juniors Bildarchiv GmbH/ Alamy, p. 23 (den); Michael DeYoung/ SuperStock, p. 23 (nursing); Gudkov Andrey, p. 23 (wrestle).

24